MONSTER FIGHT CLUB
HEROES OF MYTHS AND LEGENDS

ANITA GANERI AND DAVID WEST

PowerKiDS
press

New York

Published in 2012 by The Rosen Publishing Group, Inc.
29 East 21st Street, New York, NY 10010

Designed and produced by
David West Books

Designer and illustrator: David West
Editor: Ronne Randall
U.S. Editor: Kara Murray

Library of Congress Cataloging-in-Publication Data

Ganeri, Anita, 1961–
Heroes of myths and legends / by Anita Ganeri and David West.
p. cm. — (Monster fight club)
Includes index.
ISBN 978-1-4488-5200-0 (library binding) — ISBN 978-1-4488-5238-3 (pbk.) —
ISBN 978-1-4488-5239-0 (6-pack)
1. Heroes—Mythology—Juvenile literature. 2. Legends. I. West, David, 1956– II. Title. III. Series.
BL325.H46G36 2012
398'.45—dc22

2011005530

Manufactured in China

CPSIA Compliance Information: Batch #DS1102PK:
For Further Information contact Rosen Publishing, New York,
New York at 1-800-237-9932

CONTENTS

INTRODUCTION

Welcome to the Monster Fight Club! Watch in awe as heroes and heroines from myth and legend enter the ring to do battle. Have you ever wondered who would win—mighty Sigurd or awesome Achilles? Find out as you enter their swashbuckling world.

How Does It Work?

There are six monster fights in this book. Before each fight, you will see a profile page for each contestant. This page gives you more information about them. Once you have read the profile pages, you might be able to take a better guess at who will win the fight.

WARNING

Blood will be spilled!

The profile pages are crammed with fascinating and bloodcurdling facts about each of the contestants.

The illustrations show the contestants in some of their other gory guises.

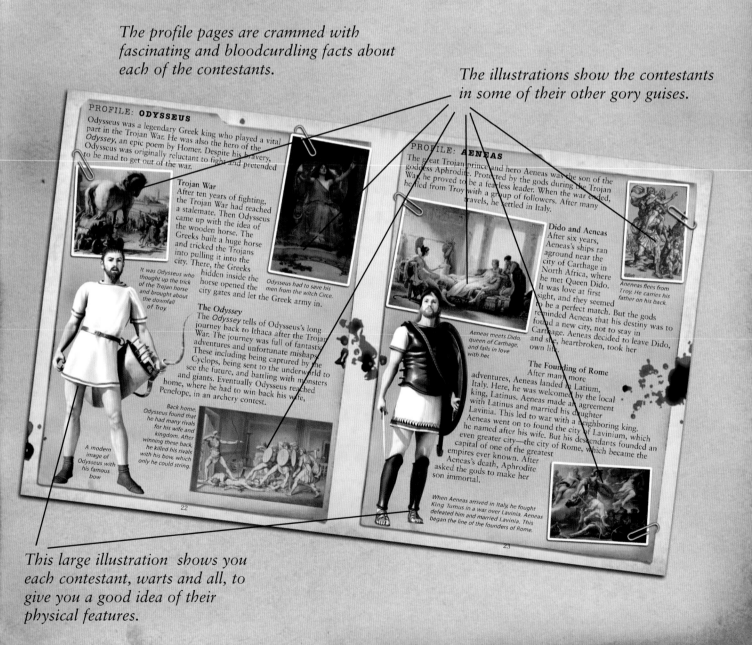

PROFILE: ODYSSEUS

Odysseus was a legendary Greek king who played a vital part in the Trojan War. He was also the hero of the *Odyssey*, an epic poem by Homer. Despite his bravery, Odysseus was originally reluctant to fight and pretended to be mad to get out of the war.

Trojan War
After ten years of fighting, the Trojan War had reached a stalemate. Then Odysseus came up with the idea of the wooden horse. The Greeks built a huge horse and tricked the Trojans into pulling it into the city. There, the Greeks hidden inside the horse opened the city gates and let the Greek army in.

It was Odysseus who thought up the trick of the Trojan horse and brought about the downfall of Troy.

Odysseus had to save his men from the witch Circe.

The Odyssey
The *Odyssey* tells of Odysseus's long journey back to Ithaca after the Trojan War. The journey was full of fantastic adventures and unfortunate mishaps. These including being captured by the Cyclops, being sent to the underworld to see the future, and battling with monsters and giants. Eventually Odysseus reached home, where he had to win back his wife, Penelope, in an archery contest.

Back home, Odysseus found that he had many rivals for his wife and kingdom. After winning these back, he killed his rivals with his bow, which only he could string.

A modern image of Odysseus with his famous bow

22

PROFILE: AENEAS

The great Trojan prince and hero Aeneas was the son of the goddess Aphrodite. Protected by the gods during the Trojan War, he proved to be a fearless leader. When the war ended, he fled from Troy with a group of followers. After many travels, he settled in Italy.

Dido and Aeneas
After six years, Aeneas's ships ran aground near the city of Carthage in North Africa, where he met Queen Dido. It was love at first sight, and they seemed to be a perfect match. But the gods reminded Aeneas that his destiny was to found a new city, not to stay in Carthage. Aeneas decided to leave Dido, and she, heartbroken, took her own life.

Aeneas meets Dido, queen of Carthage, and falls in love with her.

Aeneas flees from Troy. He carries his father on his back.

The Founding of Rome
After many more adventures, Aeneas landed in Latium, Italy. Here, he was welcomed by the local king, Latinus. Aeneas made an agreement with Latinus and married his daughter Lavinia. This led to war with a neighboring king. Aeneas went on to found the city of Lavinium, which he named after his wife. But his descendants founded an even greater city—the city of Rome, which became the capital of one of the greatest empires ever known. After Aeneas's death, Aphrodite asked the gods to make her son immortal.

When Aeneas arrived in Italy he fought King Turnus in a war over Lavinia. Aeneas defeated him and married Lavinia. This began the line of the founders of Rome.

23

This large illustration shows you each contestant, warts and all, to give you a good idea of their physical features.

In the main text, read a chilling account of how each fight progresses.

Each of the contestants may also fight under a different name, shown here as AKA (As Known As).

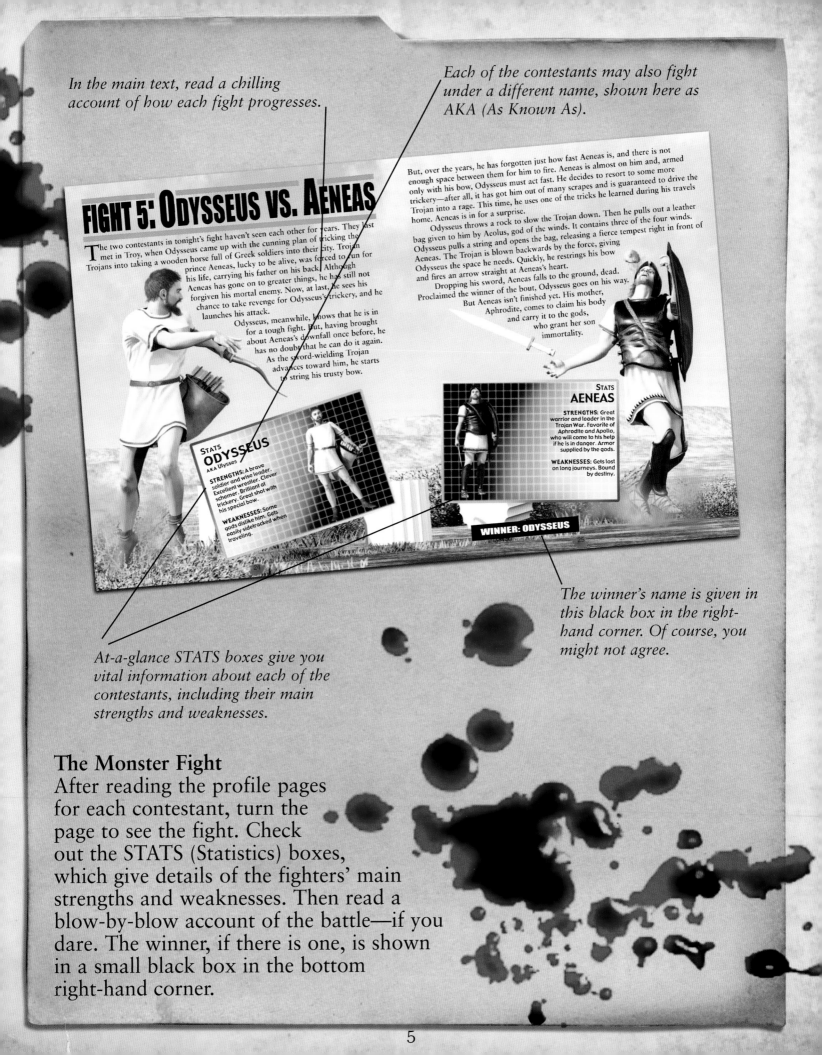

FIGHT 5: ODYSSEUS VS. AENEAS

The two contestants in tonight's fight haven't seen each other for years. They last met in Troy, when Odysseus came up with the cunning plan of tricking the Trojans into taking a wooden horse full of Greek soldiers into their city. Trojan prince Aeneas, lucky to be alive, was forced to run for his life, carrying his father on his back. Although Aeneas has gone on to greater things, he has still not forgiven his mortal enemy. Now, at last, he sees his chance to take revenge for Odysseus's trickery, and he launches his attack.

Odysseus, meanwhile, knows that he is in for a tough fight. But, having brought about Aeneas's downfall once before, he has no doubt that he can do it again. As the sword-wielding Trojan advances toward him, he starts to string his trusty bow.

But, over the years, he has forgotten just how fast Aeneas is, and there is not enough space between them for him to fire. Aeneas is almost on him and, armed only with his bow, Odysseus must act fast. He decides to resort to some more trickery—after all, it has got him out of many scrapes and is guaranteed to drive the Trojan into a rage. This time, he uses one of the tricks he learned during his travels home. Aeneas is in for a surprise.

Odysseus throws a rock to slow the Trojan down. Then he pulls out a leather bag given to him by Aeolus, god of the winds. It contains three of the four winds. Odysseus pulls a string and opens the bag, releasing a fierce tempest right in front of Aeneas. The Trojan is blown backwards by the force, giving Odysseus the space he needs. Quickly, he restrings his bow and fires an arrow straight at Aeneas's heart.

Dropping his sword, Aeneas falls to the ground, dead. Proclaimed the winner of the bout, Odysseus goes on his way. But Aeneas isn't finished yet. His mother, Aphrodite, comes to claim his body and carry it to the gods, who grant her son immortality.

STATS
ODYSSEUS
AKA Ulysses

STRENGTHS: A brave soldier and wise leader. Excellent wrestler. Clever schemer. Brilliant at trickery. Great shot with his special bow.

WEAKNESSES: Some gods dislike him. Gets easily sidetracked when traveling.

STATS
AENEAS

STRENGTHS: Great warrior and leader in the Trojan War. Favorite of Aphrodite and Apollo, who will come to his help if he is in danger. Armor supplied by the gods.

WEAKNESSES: Gets lost on long journeys. Bound by destiny.

WINNER: ODYSSEUS

At-a-glance STATS boxes give you vital information about each of the contestants, including their main strengths and weaknesses.

The winner's name is given in this black box in the right-hand corner. Of course, you might not agree.

The Monster Fight

After reading the profile pages for each contestant, turn the page to see the fight. Check out the STATS (Statistics) boxes, which give details of the fighters' main strengths and weaknesses. Then read a blow-by-blow account of the battle—if you dare. The winner, if there is one, is shown in a small black box in the bottom right-hand corner.

PROFILE: **SIGURD**

Sigurd tests his sword, Gram, by striking it against an anvil. The sword was so powerful that it cut the anvil in two.

A great hero of Norse mythology, Sigurd was brought up by the blacksmith Regin when his father died. Regin forged Sigurd a powerful sword, called Gram, then sent him out to kill the dragon Fafnir and seize the creature's gold.

Dragon Slayer

Sigurd entered the dragon's lair and killed the dragon by plunging Gram into its heart. Then he bathed in the dragon's blood. This made him invulnerable, except for a small patch on his shoulder. Sigurd also ate the dragon's heart, which gave him the gift of understanding animals. In this way, he learned from the birds that Regin was plotting to kill him and steal the gold for himself. So Sigurd killed Regin instead.

In this image, Sigurd is shown in typical Norse armor.

Sigurd and Brynhild

Later, Sigurd fell in love with the Valkyrie Brynhild and gave her a magic ring. Unknown to either of them, it brought a curse on whoever wore it. Tragedy followed. Sigurd was tricked into falling in love with a princess named Gudrun. Distraught, Brynhild had him killed, then killed herself.

Sigurd kills the dragon Fafnir by hiding in a hole in the ground and leaping out to stab it in the heart as it passes close by.

Brynhild throws herself onto Sigurd's funeral pyre.

PROFILE: ACHILLES

One of the greatest of all ancient Greek heroes, Achilles was the son of King Peleus and the nymph Thetis. A brave warrior, Achilles fought with glory in the Trojan War. The story of his deeds is told in the *Iliad*, an epic poem by Homer.

Weak Spot

When Achilles was born, Thetis tried to make him immortal by dipping him into the River Styx. The only place that the water did not touch was his heel, where Thetis was holding him. This became Achilles' weak spot, the only part of his body where he could be fatally wounded.

Achilles was brought up by the centaur Chiron.

Achilles, the great Greek warrior

The Trojan War

Achilles was a great hero of the Trojan War, fought between Troy and Greece. He avenged the death of his friend Patroclus by killing the Trojan hero Hector and dragging his body around the city behind his chariot. Achilles was finally killed by Paris, who found Achilles' weak spot and shot an arrow through his heel. After Achilles' death, a struggle broke out among the Greeks over who should inherit the great hero's armor. The armor was eventually given to Odysseus (see page 22) who handed it on to Achilles' son.

The term "Achilles' heel" has come to mean a person's weak spot. Achilles' weak spot was his heel.

FIGHT 1: SIGURD VS. ACHILLES

First up on tonight's bill are two of the greatest heroes of mythology. On the left is the mighty Sigurd, Norse dragon slayer extraordinaire. Armed with Gram, a sword that can cut clean through stone, he is a formidable opponent. Facing him is the Greek powerhouse Achilles, still smarting from the death of his close friend Patroclus and hell-bent on revenge. Achilles has chosen a short, glorious life. Will his wish come true? Both men are feared fighters and seemingly invincible. But both have their weak spots, and it is only a matter of time before they discover each other's.

Moody Achilles is sulking in his tent when Sigurd challenges him to come out and fight. Sigurd calls Achilles a coward and boasts about his own dragon slaying—killing men is easy by comparison, he laughs. Eventually Achilles can stand it no longer and rises to the bait—he hates being mocked—and the battle can begin.

STATS

SIGURD
AKA Siegfried, Sivard

STRENGTHS: Brave and strong. Owns Gram, a magic sword that can cut through metal and stone. Has the ability to understand the language of animals and can tell the future. Mostly invulnerable.

WEAKNESSES: Vulnerable to treachery and trickery. Has a weak spot on his shoulder.

Swords raised, the two warriors circle each other, waiting for the chance to strike. Both are well protected with swords and armor—Achilles' armor has been made for him by the gods. Finally Sigurd makes a move, brandishing Gram and striking a heavy blow to Achilles' arm. Achilles is shaken but unharmed, and strikes back. He hits Sigurd on the leg, but Sigurd barely registers the blow.

The battle continues for several days, with both men scoring hits but inflicting no lasting damage. Warned by the birds of Achilles' weak spot, Sigurd aims the majority of his blows at the Greek's legs but is unable to find his mark. Likewise, the gods have told Achilles to aim for Sigurd's shoulder, but he too fails to connect. With no sign of a winner, there is no choice but to call the fight a draw. Both men head off muttering about the next time and the great victory that will be theirs.

STATS
ACHILLES
AKA Achilleus

STRENGTHS: Brave and loyal. Mostly invulnerable. Has the Greek gods on his side.

WEAKNESSES: Moody and fond of sulking. Hates being mocked. Has a weak spot on his heel.

DRAW

PROFILE: HUA MULAN

In Chinese legend, Hua Mulan was a great heroine, famous for her bravery and daring. Her story is told in the Chinese poem "The Ballad of Mulan." It tells how Hua Mulan's old and ill father was recruited to join the emperor's army—an order he could not refuse. Disguising herself as a man, Hua Mulan volunteered to take her father's place.

A Soldier's Life

Legend says that Hua Mulan set off for battle with a sword inherited from her ancestors. For 12 years, she fought bravely, despite many hardships, and was regularly praised for her heroic deeds. During this time, Hua Mulan fell in love with an officer called Jin Yong, and revealed her true identity to him. The two planned to marry, but Jin Yong was killed in battle.

A modern image of Hua Mulan

A painting showing Hua Mulan on her way to war

Warriors in ancient China

Revealing Herself

After many years in the army, Hua Mulan was allowed to return home. She was summoned by the emperor, who wanted to reward her with a place at court for her outstanding service. Hua Mulan refused but accepted a horse instead. Later, when her former comrades visited her, she revealed that she was a woman.

PROFILE: **PENTHESILEA**

In Greek mythology, Penthesilea was queen of the Amazons and daughter of Ares, god of war. She accidentally killed her sister Hippolyta with a spear while they were out hunting deer. Filled with grief, she decided to end her life, but, as a great warrior, she wanted to die honorably in battle and so fought for the Trojans in the Trojan War (see below).

An Amazon with a shield and an ax

Amazons

The Amazons were female warriors in Greek mythology and were believed to live in what is now Turkey. From an early age, they were trained in hunting and warfare, and were said to be skilled fighters with spears and bows and arrows.

A modern image of Penthesilea as an Amazon warrior

After Achilles kills Penthesilea, he takes her helmet off. He is filled with regret because she is so beautiful.

Death at Troy

To make amends for the death of her sister, Penthesilea went to fight on the side of the Trojans in the Trojan War. She arrived with a band of her warriors and vowed to kill the Greek hero Achilles. On her one and only day of fighting, Penthesilea killed many Greeks before confronting Achilles, who eventually killed her, then bitterly regretted it.

FIGHT 2: HUA MULAN VS. PENTHESILEA

The scene of tonight's fight is an abandoned battlefield somewhere in the ancient world. An eerie silence surrounds our contestants—two of the most courageous female fighters in legend. Penthesilea, queen of the Amazons, is dressed for battle with a bronze helmet and brandishes a shield, sword, and spear. Her opponent, the heroine Hua Mulan, is still dressed in the armor of a male soldier. She has been wearing this uniform for so long, she cannot imagine fighting without it. Penthesilea is unaware of who Hua Mulan really is.

Penthesilea is surprised by the agility of the soldier she is facing. She has dispatched many fine fighters in her time, but this one is proving difficult to pin down. The two approach each other warily, not knowing what to expect. Then Penthesilea loses patience and lunges at Hua Mulan with her spear.

STATS
HUA MULAN
AKA Zhu Mulan

STRENGTHS: Courageous and skilled fighter. Has fought in many bloody battles. Can cope with great hardship. Martial-arts expert.

WEAKNESSES: Only flesh and blood. Unlucky in love.

12

Using nimble martial-arts footwork, Hua Mulan dodges deftly out of the way. Penthesilea tries again, but this time Hua Mulan knocks the spear out of her hand with a well-aimed kick. Stunned by her opponent's unusual tactics, Penthesilea is unsure what to do. She quickly recovers, however, when Hua Mulan rushes toward her with her halberd.

The fight continues with many twists and turns, until Penthesilea manages to knock Hua Mulan's helmet off, revealing her true identity. Penthesilea is shocked to find that she is fighting a woman, and immediately drops her sword. Still grief-stricken at the killing of Hippolyta, she refuses to continue fighting. With her opponent an easy target, victory is now well within Hua Mulan's grasp. She knocks Penthesilea to the ground, raises her halberd, and prepares to strike. At the last moment, however, Hua Mulan changes her mind. She spares Penthesilea's life and allows her to go on her way.

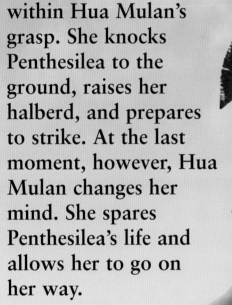

STATS
PENTHESILEA
AKA Queen of the Amazons

STRENGTHS: Fearless warrior. Daughter of a god.

WEAKNESSES: Grief-stricken by death of sister. Easily killed by Achilles.

WINNER: HUA MULAN

A legendary king of Britain, Arthur is believed to have lived in the Dark Ages (5th–6th centuries). Famous for his skill in battle, he was seen as a just ruler and great warrior who defended Britain against the Saxons, who were trying to invade.

Knights of the Round Table

At his court in Camelot, Arthur gathered the greatest knights in the country to sit around his famous round table. Because of its shape, everyone sitting around it was considered to be equal. Among the knights were the dashing Sir Lancelot, Arthur's greatest friend, noble Sir Perceval, and the daring Sir Galahad, who led the quest for the Holy Grail.

Excalibur, Arthur's sword, was said to have a magical scabbard that protected its wearer from harm. It was stolen by Arthur's sister, Morgan le Fay.

Camelot was the name of the famous castle at the center of Arthur's court. Its location is uncertain and is still debated to this day.

Arthur's Last Battle

In Arthur's final battle at Camlann, he was badly wounded by his evil nephew and rival to the throne, Mordred. Close to death, Arthur was taken by boat to the magical island of Avalon, where it is said that his soul lives on.

In the final battle, Arthur kills Mordred but is fatally wounded.

PROFILE: **PERSEUS**

The Greek hero Perseus was the son of the god Zeus and Princess Danae. Danae's father was warned that his grandson would kill him, so he set Perseus and Danae adrift in a wooden chest. They were rescued by King Polydectes of Seriphos.

Perseus with Medusa's head

Killing Medusa

One day, Polydectes set Perseus a challenge. To prove his courage, he was to bring the king a gift—the head of Medusa, a hideous Gorgon whose gaze could turn people to stone. The gods gave Perseus a shining shield, a sickle, winged sandals, and a helmet that made the wearer invisible. Perseus used the shield as a mirror so that he did not have to look at Medusa directly. Then he cut off her head with the sickle.

Medusa had snakes instead of hair.

Perseus falls in love with Andromeda after rescuing her.

Perseus and Andromeda

Flying home on his winged sandals, Perseus saw Andromeda chained to a rock. She was about to be sacrificed to a sea monster. Perseus killed the monster and rescued her. In return, her grateful father agreed that Perseus and Andromeda could be married. Later, Perseus took part in some games. As he threw a discus, it was blown off course and killed an old man. The old man was Perseus's grandfather (see above).

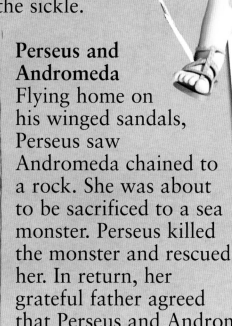

Many of the stories about Perseus tell of him using Medusa's head to turn people to stone.

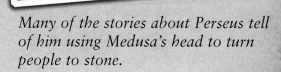

On his journey back from slaying Medusa, Perseus happens across a much more puzzling opponent. King Arthur has lost his way on his latest quest, and now finds himself facing the Gorgon slayer. Neither contestant knows anything about the other. They have no idea of each other's strengths and weaknesses, but they are going to have to learn fast.

Arthur hears a strange, whooshing sound above him. He looks up to see Perseus hovering on his winged sandals. He pulls down the visor of his helmet and, taking Excalibur out of its magic scabbard, raises it into the air and charges toward his foe. But Perseus is ready. He lifts up his shield so that it catches the rays of the sun. Arthur is dazzled by the blinding light, and in his confusion he drops Excalibur. As he stoops to pick up the sword, Perseus lashes out with his sickle. Arthur catches a glancing blow. Unharmed, because he is wearing Excalibur's scabbard, Arthur regroups and plans to relaunch his attack.

STATS

KING ARTHUR
AKA Arthur Pendragon

STRENGTHS: Magic sword and scabbard that can heal wounds. Great leader and soldier. Famous sense of fairness.

WEAKNESSES: Can be overcome by the forces of evil. Can be betrayed.

PERSEUS

AKA Perseus Eurymedon

STRENGTHS: Has winged sandals that allow him to fly and a helmet of invisibility. Helped by the gods.

WEAKNESSES: Can be boastful. Can be lethal when throwing the discus.

But, looking around, he cannot see Perseus anywhere. The Greek has disappeared by putting on his helmet of invisibility. Bound by his code of chivalry, Arthur does not think that this makes for a fair fight and tells Perseus (wherever he is) this. Perseus agrees not to use the helmet again, but he has another, much deadlier, trick left up his sleeve. Just as Arthur seems to be gaining the upper hand with his superior swordsmanship, Perseus unleashes his greatest weapon yet. He drops his shield and with a flourish, he produces the head of Medusa, which he has been carrying in a special bag. From that moment on, there can be no doubt about who will win the fight. As soon as Arthur sets eyes on Medusa, he is turned to stone.

WINNER: PERSEUS

PROFILE: ROSTAM

The greatest of all Persian heroes was called Rostam. The son of a legendary warrior and a princess, he was famed for his courage and strength. He rode a mighty stallion, called Rakhsh, that he had tamed when he was only a young child.

Book of Kings

The *Shahnama* (Book of Kings) is a very long Persian poem written in around AD 1000. It tells the story of Persia's past and of its heroes, including Rostam. One famous story tells how Rostam fatally wounded Sohrab in battle, unaware that Sohrab was his son.

Rostam defeats Esfandyr by shooting him in the eye, his only weak spot.

Rostam's Labors

Legend says that Rostam's king was captured and blinded by demons and that Rostam vowed to rescue him. He had to perform a series of tasks, known as the Seven Labors. These included killing ferocious lions and dragons, with the help of his faithful horse, Rakhsh. Eventually, as his seventh and final labor, Rostam overthrew the demons and rescued the king. He used the blood of the demon chief to restore the king's sight.

Rostam and his legendary horse, Rakhsh

Rostam mourns Sohrab after killing him in battle. He discovered that Sohrab was his son only after he had fatally wounded him.

Herakles, or Hercules, was the son of Zeus and Princess Alcmene. Half god, half mortal, Herakles grew up to have extraordinary strength. Zeus's wife, Hera, made Herakles' life difficult because he reminded her of Zeus's affair. When he was a baby, she sent two serpents to his cradle to kill him. But, surprising everyone with his strength, Herakles killed them instead. Hera vowed to seek revenge.

As a baby, Herakles killed two snakes.

Twelve Labors

When Herakles got married and had children, Hera seized her chance. She drove Herakles mad so that he killed his family in a dreadful rage. When Herakles recovered, he was horrified and wanted to make amends. So King Eurystheus gave him twelve, seemingly impossible, tasks. They included having to kill a lion with a skin so tough no weapon could pierce it. Then Herakles had to kill the Hydra, a monster that grew two heads every time one head was cut off. Later, Herakles had to capture the vicious, three-headed dog Cerberus. Herakles completed every task and was finally freed from his terrible guilt.

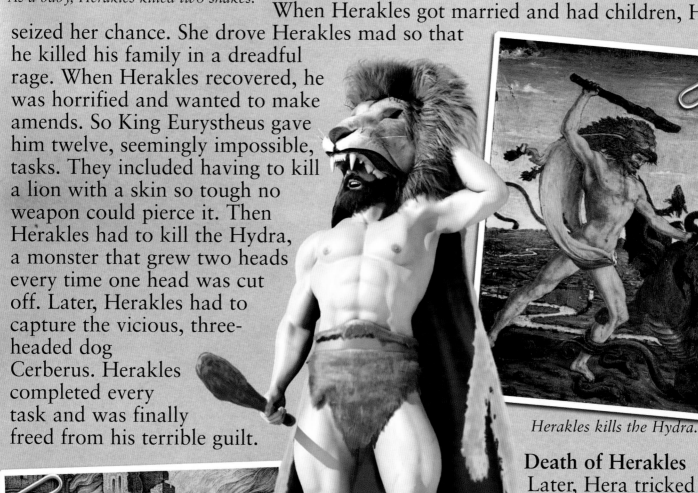

Herakles kills the Hydra.

Herakles tames Cerberus.

Death of Herakles

Later, Hera tricked Herakles into wearing a poisoned shirt. In agony, he had a funeral pyre built and climbed on it to die. But Zeus pulled him from the fire and granted him immortality.

FIGHT 4: ROSTAM VS. HERAKLES

In tonight's fight, two true heavyweights are pitted against each other. Separated by location and history, they have never met before, yet they have plenty in common. Both are immensely brave. Both have superhuman strength. Both have succeeded in performing a series of seemingly impossible tasks that would have had mere mortals quaking in their boots. No one knows how this bout will end, but it is going to be a very close call.

Rostam rides into battle on Rakhsh, his faithful stallion. At the sight of Herakles, Rakhsh suddenly rears up, snorting wildly, and almost unseats his rider. Rostam tries to steady his horse but then realizes what has spooked him. Herakles is wearing the skin of the Nemean lion and is a fearsome sight. Rakhsh gets ready to charge—he has dispatched a monstrous lion before— but Rostam holds him back. He needs a moment to reflect on his opponent—the likes of whom he has never seen before.

Herakles has no such qualms. He raises his mighty club and goes in for the kill, taking Rostam by surprise. He succeeds in knocking Rostam off his horse, though Rostam quickly recovers and picks up his mace. Managing to avoid many of Herakles' blows, Rostam brings the mace down on the Greek's back. As a child, he killed an elephant with one blow, but he has no such success this time. The lion-skin cloak does its job, and the mace simply bounces off, leaving Herakles unharmed.

Famous for his own strength and courage, Rostam realizes that he has met his match. He is fighting an unbeatable foe, and will be lucky to escape with his life. As Herakles prepares to relaunch his attack, Rostam thinks fast. Swallowing his pride, he uses the moment to remount Rakhsh and gallops away as quickly as possible.

PROFILE: **ODYSSEUS**

Odysseus was a legendary Greek king who played a vital part in the Trojan War. He was also the hero of the *Odyssey*, an epic poem by Homer. Despite his bravery, Odysseus was originally reluctant to fight and pretended to be mad to get out of the war.

Trojan War

After ten years of fighting, the Trojan War had reached a stalemate. Then Odysseus came up with the idea of the wooden horse. The Greeks built a huge horse and tricked the Trojans into pulling it into the city. There, the Greeks hidden inside the horse opened the city gates and let the Greek army in.

It was Odysseus who thought up the trick of the Trojan horse and brought about the downfall of Troy.

Odysseus had to save his men from the witch Circe.

The *Odyssey*

The *Odyssey* tells of Odysseus's long journey back to Ithaca after the Trojan War. The journey was full of fantastic adventures and unfortunate mishaps. These included being captured by the Cyclops, being sent to the underworld to see the future, and battling with monsters and giants. Eventually Odysseus reached home, where he had to win back his wife, Penelope, in an archery contest.

A modern image of Odysseus with his famous bow

Back home, Odysseus found that he had many rivals for his wife and kingdom. After winning these back, he killed his rivals with his bow, which only he could string.

PROFILE: **AENEAS**

The great Trojan prince and hero Aeneas was the son of the goddess Aphrodite. Protected by the gods during the Trojan War, he proved to be a fearless leader. When the war ended, he fled from Troy with a group of followers. After many travels, he settled in Italy.

Aneneas flees from Troy. He carries his father on his back.

Aeneas meets Dido, queen of Carthage, and falls in love with her.

Dido and Aeneas

After six years, Aeneas's ships ran aground near the city of Carthage in North Africa, where he met Queen Dido. It was love at first sight, and they seemed to be a perfect match. But the gods reminded Aeneas that his destiny was to found a new city, not to stay in Carthage. Aeneas decided to leave Dido, and she, heartbroken, took her own life.

The Founding of Rome

After many more adventures, Aeneas landed in Latium, Italy. Here, he was welcomed by the local king, Latinus. Aeneas made an agreement with Latinus and married his daughter Lavinia. This led to war with a neighboring king. Aeneas went on to found the city of Lavinium, which he named after his wife. But his descendants founded an even greater city—the city of Rome, which became the capital of one of the greatest empires ever known. After Aeneas's death, Aphrodite asked the gods to make her son immortal.

When Aeneas arrived in Italy, he fought King Turnus in a war over Lavinia. Aeneas defeated him and married Lavinia. This began the line of the founders of Rome.

FIGHT 5: ODYSSEUS VS. AENEAS

The two contestants in tonight's fight haven't seen each other for years. They last met in Troy, when Odysseus came up with the cunning plan of tricking the Trojans into taking a wooden horse full of Greek soldiers into their city. Trojan prince Aeneas, lucky to be alive, was forced to run for his life, carrying his father on his back. Although Aeneas has gone on to greater things, he has still not forgiven his mortal enemy. Now, at last, he sees his chance to take revenge for Odysseus's trickery, and he launches his attack.

Odysseus, meanwhile, knows that he is in for a tough fight. But, having brought about Aeneas's downfall once before, he has no doubt that he can do it again. As the sword-wielding Trojan advances toward him, he starts to string his trusty bow.

STATS
ODYSSEUS
AKA Ulysses

STRENGTHS: A brave soldier and wise leader. Excellent wrestler. Clever schemer. Brilliant at trickery. Great shot with his special bow.

WEAKNESSES: Some gods dislike him. Gets easily sidetracked when traveling.

But, over the years, he has forgotten just how fast Aeneas is, and there is not enough space between them for him to fire. Aeneas is almost on him and, armed only with his bow, Odysseus must act fast. He decides to resort to some more trickery—after all, it has got him out of many scrapes and is guaranteed to drive the Trojan into a rage. This time, he uses one of the tricks he learned during his travels home. Aeneas is in for a surprise.

Odysseus throws a rock to slow the Trojan down. Then he pulls out a leather bag given to him by Aeolus, god of the winds. It contains three of the four winds. Odysseus pulls a string and opens the bag, releasing a fierce tempest right in front of Aeneas. The Trojan is blown backwards by the force, giving Odysseus the space he needs. Quickly, he restrings his bow and fires an arrow straight at Aeneas's heart.

Dropping his sword, Aeneas falls to the ground, dead. Proclaimed the winner of the bout, Odysseus goes on his way. But Aeneas isn't finished yet. His mother, Aphrodite, comes to claim his body and carry it to the gods, who grant her son immortality.

STATS
AENEAS

STRENGTHS: Great warrior and leader in the Trojan War. Favorite of Aphrodite and Apollo, who will come to his help if he is in danger. Armor supplied by the gods.

WEAKNESSES: Gets lost on long journeys. Bound by destiny.

WINNER: ODYSSEUS

PROFILE: DOBRYNYA NIKITICH

Famous for his courage, Dobrynya Nikitich was a great hero and warrior of Russian legend. Stories of his exploits, told in epic poems, were passed on by word of mouth.

Heroic Features

Legend says that Dobrynya was a warlord at the court of Prince Vladimir I. He was often sent on difficult and dangerous missions by the prince. Besides being courageous, Dobrynya was skilled at archery and wrestling, and was an excellent musician.

Three great Russian heroes—Dobrynya Nikitich, Ilya Muromets, and Alyosha Popovich

Slaying a Dragon

In one story, a dragon called Gorynch, from the Saracen Mountains, captured the niece of Prince Vladimir. Dobrynya had battled the dragon once before, and the prince now called on him to rescue the princess. Dobrynya made his way to the mountains with the help of a magic whip. After three days of fighting, he killed Gorynch, but he and his horse got stuck in the dragon's blood. Then he heard a voice telling him to stick his spear in the ground and say a spell to set them free.

Dobrynya Nikitich rescues a princess from the dragon Gorynch.

26

PROFILE: **BEOWULF**

Beowulf was the hero of an epic poem of the same name, written in Old English. A great warrior, he belonged to a people called the Geats, who lived in southern Sweden. Dressed in his magic chain mail shirt, which protected him in battle, Beowulf became famous for slaying monsters that were terrorizing his own country and places farther away. Beowulf became king of the Geats and had a long and successful reign.

Beowulf killed Grendel without using any weapons.

Monster Slayer

Early on, Beowulf traveled to Denmark, where a monster, called Grendel, was attacking the king's palace. Beowulf fought Grendel and killed him in unarmed combat. The Danes began to celebrate, but they were not safe yet. The next night, Grendel's mother came to take revenge for her son's death. Beowulf tracked her down to her lair by a lake. He could not kill her with his own sword. Instead, he took one of her own swords and cut her head off with it.

Beowulf wearing his magical armor.

Grendel's mother could not pierce Beowulf's magic armor.

The Last Fight

When Beowulf was an old man, a dragon attacked his kingdom. Beowulf set off to fight it. Most of his warriors fled in fear, except for the faithful Wiglaf. Together they killed the dragon, but Beowulf was fatally poisoned by the dragon's breath, and died.

Beowulf hides from the dragon's fiery breath behind a shield.

FIGHT 6: DOBRYNYA NIKITICH VS.

The final fight of the night takes place in dragon country, where the landscape is pitted with fire and molten rock. Against this dramatic background, two of the greatest dragon slayers of legend have met for a sensational showdown. Both are mighty warriors, dressed in armor and wielding mighty swords. Both are famous for their strength and courage, and both like to boast about their exploits. They start with some friendly banter about the number of dragons each has slain, but the time quickly comes for the boasting to stop and the fighting to begin.

The fight continues for several hours—our contestants are well matched. In fierce, hand-to-hand combat, they trade blow after blow. Thanks to his magic armor, Beowulf is well protected and gains the advantage. Frustrated that he is not making any headway, Dobrynya is about to give up when he hears a voice telling him not to be a coward and to keep fighting for his life. The Russian relaunches his attack, but he is beaten back by Beowulf. Dobrynya prepares to meet his doom when the fight takes an unexpected turn.

STATS
DOBRYNYA NIKITICH

STRENGTHS: Good at archery and wrestling. Known for his courage and cunning. Has a magic whip. Hears voices that give him advice.

WEAKNESSES: Sometimes makes deals with dragons. Can get stuck in dragon's blood.

BEOWULF

STATS

BEOWULF
AKA King of the Geats

STRENGTHS: Fearless dragon slayer. Wears armor that cannot be pierced. Can wield a huge sword.

WEAKNESSES: Fatally allergic to a dragon's bad breath.

WINNER: DOBRYNYA NIKITICH

Just as Beowulf is about to strike the fatal blow, he stops and looks around. Then he sniffs the air. A foul, sulfurous smell fills his nostrils—a sure sign that a dragon is nearby. While Dobrynya looks on in astonishment, Beowulf turns his back on the fight and sets off in hot pursuit. He cannot resist the temptation to slay one more dragon and is even willing to forfeit the fight for the chance to do so. Dobrynya picks himself up, dusts himself off, and breathes a sigh of relief. Declared the winner by default, he knows only too well that he has had a very lucky escape.

CREATE YOUR OWN FIGHT

You might not agree with some of the fight results in this book. If that's the case, try writing up your own fight report based on the facts supplied on the prefight profile pages. Better still, choose your own heroes and heroines and create your own fight.

Monster Research

Once you have chosen your two heroes or heroines, do some research about them using books and the Internet. You can make them fairly similar, like Dobrynya Nikitich and Beowulf, or quite different, like Rostam and Herakles.

Stats Boxes

Think about stats for each hero or heroine. Find out about any other names for the AKA section. Make a list of strengths, such as how powerful they are and if they have magic armor or use secret weapons, and also list any weaknesses.

In the Ring

Pick a setting where your heroes or heroines are likely to meet, and write a blow-by-blow account of how you imagine the fight might happen. Think about each contestant's key characteristics, along with his or her strengths and weaknesses. Remember, there doesn't always have to be a winner.

Heroes of Myths and Legends

Here is a list of some other mythical heroes who might qualify for membership in the Monster Fight Club:

Ahaiyuta
Ajax
Arjuna
Bellerophon
Bhima
Bran the Blessed
Cuchulainn
Diomedes
Finn McCool
Gilgamesh
Haymo the Giant
Horatius
Jason and the Argonauts
Lancelot
Prince Cadmus
Sinbad the Sailor
Susanoo
Theseus

Theseus was a great Greek hero who killed many monsters, including the famous Minotaur.

GLOSSARY

avenged (uh-VENJD)
Inflicted a punishment in return for harm or injury done to a person.

blacksmith (BLAK-smith)
A person who works with metal and turns it into objects such as horseshoes, and weapons such as swords.

chain mail (CHAYN MAYL)
Rows of metal links or rings that are used to make a flexible type of armor.

immortal (ih-MAWR-tul)
Never dying but living forever.

invulnerable (in-VUL-neh-ruh-bel)
Not able to be wounded, hurt, or damaged.

legendary (LEH-jen-der-ee)
Connected to legends, traditional stories that are often based on events that are supposedly historical.

mortal (MOR-tul)
Being human and, therefore, not living forever.

mythology (mih-THAH-luh-jee)
A collection of myths, or traditional stories, that use supernatural characters to explain human behavior and natural events.

nymphs (NIMFS)
Spirits of nature in ancient Greek mythology who often appeared as beautiful young women.

pyre (PY-er)
A pile of wood that is used for burning a dead body. Also called a funeral pyre.

scabbard (SKA-berd)
A holder for a weapon, such as a sword.

sickle (SIH-kul)
A tool with a short handle and curved blade that is normally used for cutting grass and crops.

stalemate (STAYL-mayt)
A situation in which two opponents find neither of them can take any further action or that further action is pointless.

stallion (STAL-yun)
A male horse.

INDEX

Web Sites

Due to the changing nature of Internet links, PowerKids Press has developed an online list of Web sites related to the subject of this book. This site is updated regularly. Please use this link to access the list:
www.powerkidslinks.com/mfc/heroes/